"All the President's Men and Women"

The Secretary of Defense
through
Les Aspin

Bob Italia

Published by Abdo & Daughters, 4940 Viking Dr., Suite 622, Edina, MN 55435.

Library bound edition distributed by Rockbottom Books, Pentagon Tower, P.O. Box 36036, Minneapolis, Minnesota 55435.

Cover Photo by: Black Star.
Inside Photos by: The Bettmann Archive.

Edited By: Rosemary Wallner

Library of Congress Cataloging–in–Publication Data
Italia, Robert, 1955-
    Les Aspin : Secretary of Defense / written by Bob Italia ; [edited by Rosemary Wallner].
          p.   cm — (All the Presidents men and women)
    Includes bibliographical references and index.
    Summary: Looks at the former representative from Wisconsin who was named Defense Secretary by President Clinton. Mentions major issues facing the military, and includes brief profiles of some former Defense Secretaries.
    ISBN 1-56239-252-2
    1. Aspin, Les—Juvenile literature. 2. Cabinet officers—United States—Biography—Juvenile literature. 3. United States. Dept. of Defense—Biography—Juvenile literature. [1. Aspin, Les. 2. Cabinet officers.] I. Wallner, Rosemary, 1964— . II. Title. III. Series.
U53.A87I82   1993
353.6' 092—dc20   93-28145
[B]   CIP
                                              AC

Contents

The President's Cabinet: An Overview

When someone is elected President of the United States, he or she immediately takes on a huge amount of responsibility. Presidents must oversee all laws passed by Congress. They are the head of the armed forces. They must decide foreign policy—how the United States should help its friends and allies, and how we should punish our enemies.

If the economy stumbles, the President must try to get it back on the right track. Presidents must make sure that laws are handed down fairly; energy is used wisely; parks and other government lands are put to proper use; citizens are educated, put to work, and kept healthy. And that is just a small part of what Presidents do.

No one person, no matter how smart, can possibly know everything there is to know to do a President's job. A President paints in broad strokes—he or she decides the tone and direction of how the country should go. To help with the details, the President has a cabinet—a group of people he or she meets with regularly who advise on important decisions that must be made every day.

There's no law that says the President must have a cabinet. It's a system that has evolved by custom over the years. The U.S. Constitution says that the President "may require the opinion, in writing, of the principal officer in each of the executive departments, upon any subject relating to the duties of their respective offices." But the President does not have to ask their advice. And the President does not have to go along with what they say if she or he thinks they are wrong.

The heads of these cabinet departments are called secretaries. The President appoints them. The Senate will then check the secretary's background and vote on whether to accept the nominee. Nominees are picked for their experience and special talents in the areas they will oversee. Only rarely is a President's pick rejected. After the Senate confirms (accepts) cabinet secretaries, the President alone has the right to remove them if he or she is unhappy with the way they are performing their duties.

President Bill Clinton presides over his first Cabinet meeting in the Cabinet Room of the White House.

The Secretary of Defense

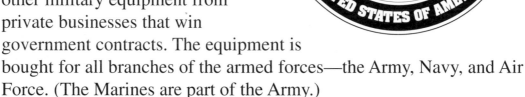

The Secretary of Defense is one of the most important and difficult cabinet positions. The Secretary is in charge of keeping America's military strong so it can defend itself against its enemies. He or she buys aircraft, tanks, guns, and other military equipment from private businesses that win government contracts. The equipment is bought for all branches of the armed forces—the Army, Navy, and Air Force. (The Marines are part of the Army.)

The Secretary of Defense also pays the military personnel (2.9 million military and civilian) and provides health care benefits. The Department usually gets more than one quarter ($274 billion) of the entire national budget. No other Department receives as much money.

The Secretary of the Defense reports to the President, who is the Commander in Chief of all armed forces. From offices in the Pentagon Building in Washington, D.C., the Secretary directs the Army, Navy, and Air Force, the Joint Chiefs of Staff (the Joint Chiefs give military advice), and other defense agencies. The Secretary also controls the schools where military officers are trained: the U.S. Military Academy, the U.S. Naval Academy, and the U.S. Air Force Academy.

Les Aspin

When Les Aspin was a young congressman, he ruffled the feathers of the military by accusing it of wasteful spending and mismanagement. Now—as President Bill Clinton's Defense Secretary—Aspin finds himself in a position to finally do something about it. His goal is to downsize by one-third the most powerful military machine in the world—without reducing its punch. "It's a huge job," said former Secretary of State Alexander Haig. "A very high-risk job. But he [Aspin] is a fighter, highly motivated, and very intelligent."

Les Aspin when he was Chairman of the House Armed Services Committee (January 30, 1986).

Leslie (Les) Aspin, Jr., was born on July 21, 1938. His father had immigrated from Yorkshire, England, to Wisconsin. Aspin attended Yale University in Boston, Massachusetts. There he joined the Reserve Officers Training Corps (ROTC). After graduating, Aspin went to Oxford University in England where he earned another degree. Then he received a doctorate in economics at the Massachusetts Institute of Technology (MIT).

The Whiz Kid

After MIT, Aspin began his career as a military specialist. During President Lyndon Johnson's administration in the 1960s, Aspin worked in the Office of Systems Analysis for former Defense Secretary Robert S. McNamara. There he became known as a "whiz kid" because of his intelligence and ability to learn quickly.

In 1970, Aspin was elected to the House of Representatives at the age of 32. He then assumed a place on the House Armed Services Committee.

Aspin strongly criticized wasteful military spending. One of his early concerns was something called "Peticare." Peticare provided health care for military officers' pets at government expense. Slowly, Aspin turned his attention to bigger issues like President Ronald Reagan's MX missile proposal and the Persian Gulf War.

Les Aspin

Born: July 21, 1938.

Position: Defense secretary

Salary: $148,400

Number of employees: 2.9 million military and civilian

Annual budget: $247 billion

Background: Elected to 11 terms as U.S. representative from Wisconsin. Former chairman of the Armed Services Committee.

Experience: Pentagon economist under Robert McNamara in the 1960s; served in the U.S. Army.

The House Armed Services Committee

Five years after his election to Congress, Aspin helped organize the ouster of Representative F. Edward Herbert of Louisiana. Herbert was the chairman of the House Armed Services Committee. Representative Melvin Price of Illinois replaced Herbert. Ten years later, Aspin helped remove Price and secured the chairmanship for himself.

As chairman, Aspin used the panel to conduct a wide range of inquires on military policy. He sought new visions of how military power should be used and what the structure of the military should be.

Clinton's Choice

Aspin was President Clinton's first choice for Secretary of Defense. Clinton met with Aspin in December 1992 to discuss the nomination. Aspin's record and reputation were strong. In January 1993, he became one of the first cabinet nominees to be approved by Congress.

Aspin worked many long hours preparing the difficult 1994 Defense budget and reshaping his department. He stated his case for use of force in Bosnia.

Les Aspin pounds the gavel as the House Armed Services Committee prepares to vote on a crucial defense issue.

Heart Problems

On February 21, 1993, Aspin was hospitalized at Georgetown University Medical Center in Washington, D.C., after suffering shortness of breath, fever, and nausea. His illness was related to his previous heart condition. (In 1991, Aspin was diagnosed with a heart condition called hypertrophic cardiomyopathy—the thickening of the heart muscle. Though not life-threatening if treated, the condition impairs the heart's ability to pump blood.)

Aspin was released from the hospital on February 25. His cardiologist said that he and other doctors at the center had recommended that Aspin have a pacemaker installed. He also advised Aspin to reduce his workload and to give up playing squash and tennis.

Aspin's health crisis caused concern at the Defense Department. There was no immediate assistant whom the secretary could transfer his duties.

Hours after leaving the hospital, Aspin returned to work at the Pentagon. He was faced with too many crucial policy decisions and could not stay away from work.

On March 16, Aspin was hospitalized with a bronchial infection. He had complained of a cough and shortness of breath. On March 18, the defense secretary was given a pacemaker to relieve the symptoms of his heart condition. (A pacemaker is about the size of a silver dollar. It was implanted near the collar bone.) The heart condition was not expected to interfere with Aspin's ability to oversee military operations. He spent a few days in the hospital to recuperate, then was back on the job once more.

Defense Secretary Les Aspin and President Bill Clinton at a February 10, 1993, cabinet meeting.

Trimming the Fat

By the end of March, Aspin finished his long-awaited 1994 budget. The major cuts came by reducing the active-duty force to 1.62 million people. The Army would have 540,000, the Navy 480,800, the Air Force 425,700, and the Marines 174,100. The cuts also reduced the Army from 14 divisions to 12. It dropped the Navy's aircraft carrier fleet from 14 to 12 and ship strength from 443 to 413. And it reduced the Air Force from 28 wings to 24.

The cuts caused controversy because Aspin also wanted to close several military bases. A total of 31 bases would be shut down and 134 would be downsized to fit a five-year, 22 percent reduction in U.S. forces. South Carolina, Florida, and California took the biggest hits. They had naval bases which Aspin targeted the hardest. He wants to reduce the 450-ship fleet to 350 by the year 2000. The closings were part of an effort to slice $122 billion over four years from the Pentagon's $262 billion annual budget.

Les Aspin answers questions about military policy from the media after a long meeting with President Clinton.

Surprisingly, Aspin did not cut costly weapons-development programs such as the Osprey tilt-rotor aircraft, the Seawolf submarine, and the C-17 transport aircraft. Aspin also recommended humanitarian

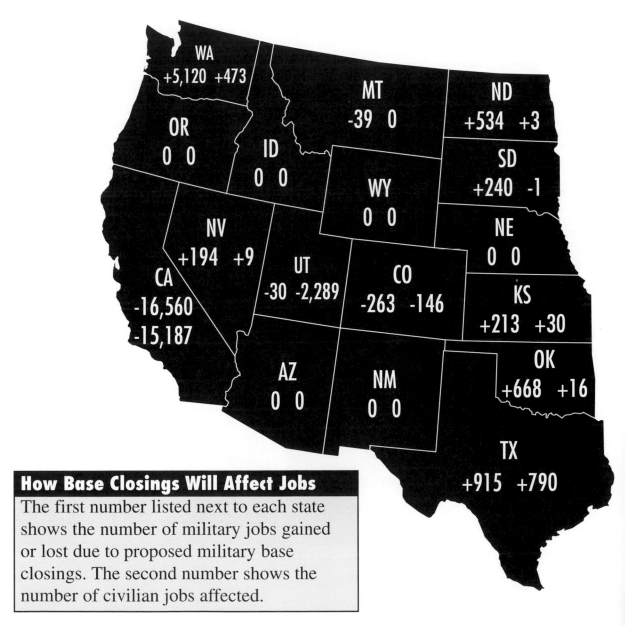

How Base Closings Will Affect Jobs

The first number listed next to each state shows the number of military jobs gained or lost due to proposed military base closings. The second number shows the number of civilian jobs affected.

"peacekeeping missions" in places like Somalia (where a civil war was creating mass starvation) and assistance in dismantling the former Soviet Union's nuclear arsenal.

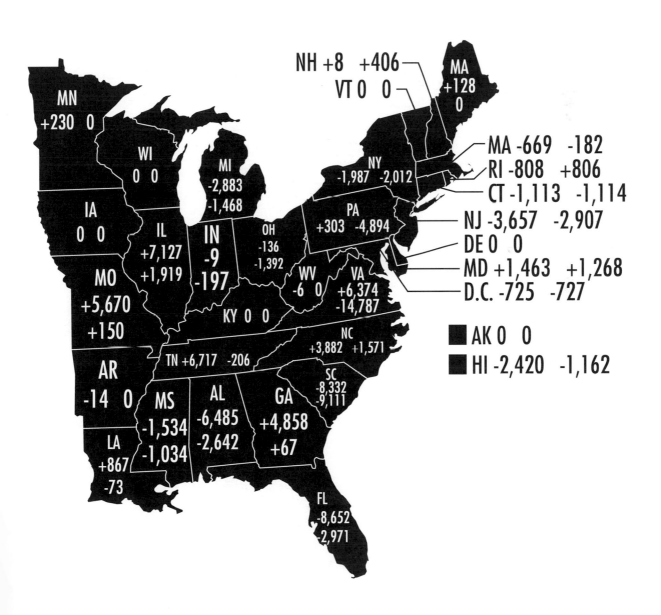

Other Issues

Following is a list of other issues Aspin will face in the coming years:

✈ Determining military policy in the trouble spots of the world. Aspin favors the use of force in Bosnia-Herzegovina where Serbians and Muslims are fighting for control. Aspin is also expected to take a hard stance against Iraq and its leader, Saddam Hussein.

✈ Examining major weapons systems. The Strategic Defense Initiative (SDI), the Seawolf submarine, and the B-2 bomber are some of the programs that have been criticized for their costs, which run into billions of dollars.

✈ Looking at domestic employment for the armed forces, which may help build roads and repair bridges.

✈ Trying to keep the defense industry healthy during a time of budget cuts.

Les Aspin will decide the fate of the B-2 Stealth bomber program.

Aspin also believes that the Soviet Union Cold War threat has been replaced by four possible dangers to U.S. security:

1) regional wars
2) the development of nuclear weapons by other countries
3) reversal of reforms in Russia
4) economic worries in America

In the future, he will be forming defense policies to combat these perceived threats.

Les Aspin is a policymaker with a vision. In the last three years, no one has more accurately projected the future of the military. During his term, he will use his knowledge of government and his clout in Congress to shrink the military while maintaining its technical superiority and quality of its all-volunteer force.

Military experts were surprised when Les Aspin spared the Seawolf submarine program from budget cuts. But its future is still in doubt.

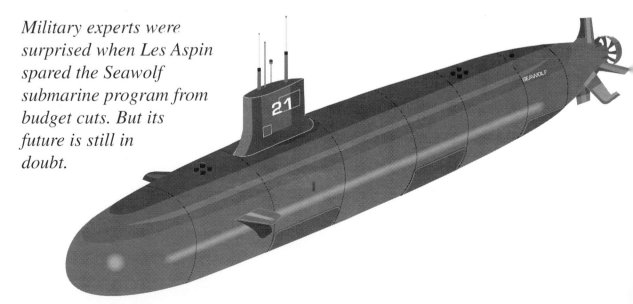

Former Defense Secretaries

James V. Forrestal
(September 17, 1947—March 27, 1949)

James V. Forrestal was born in Beacon, New York, on February 15, 1892. He was the son of an Irish immigrant who ran a construction company in the United States. Forrestal went to Princeton University in 1912. In 1916, he joined William A. Read & Company as a bond salesman. By 1938, he became president of the company.

President Franklin Roosevelt asked Forrestal to come to the White House to help organize American industry for World War II. In August 1940, Roosevelt appointed Forrestal as Under Secretary of the Navy. On May 19, 1944, he became the Secretary of the Navy before becoming the first Secretary of Defense.

Forrestal understood the threat of Soviet communism. He argued that the United States needed a variety of land, sea, and air forces to thwart the Soviet threat—not just the atomic bomb. He also pushed for economic aid to rebuild Europe after the war.

In the late 1940s, Forrestal had bouts with mental illness. He was shocked when President Harry S. Truman called him to the Oval Office in the White House and asked for his resignation. In May 1949, Forrestal fell to his death from a window on the sixteenth floor of the Bethesda, Maryland, Naval Medical Center main building. His closest friends believed he committed suicide.

*James Vincent Forrestal (1892–1949) was America's first
Secretary of Defense.*

Robert S. McNamara
(January 21, 1961—February 29, 1968)

Robert S. McNamara was born in San Francisco on June 9, 1916. His father was the sales manager of a wholesale shoe firm. McNamara graduated from the University of California at Berkeley in 1937 with degrees in economics and philosophy. He obtained a master's degree from Harvard Graduate School of Business Administration in 1939.

McNamara failed the physical examination to get into the military after the start of World War II. But he volunteered and was accepted to do logistical work, bomb loadings, and other kinds of statistical work for the Army Air Corps bomber commands in England. By 1943, he was appointed captain. After the war, McNamara joined Ford Motor Company as a manager. One day after John F. Kennedy was elected President, McNamara became president of the company.

Kennedy nominated McNamara to help make the Defense Department more efficient. McNamara quickly launched a number of programs and projects to "get things done twice as fast as they are being done presently."

McNamara served as Secretary of Defense longer than any other nominee. He worked through the 1962 Cuban Missile Crisis and the turbulent years of the Vietnam War. Because he felt McNamara had "lost his stomach for the fight," President Lyndon Johnson found another job for McNamara in 1968—as president of the World Bank. McNamara served there for several years until he retired.

Robert S. McNamara shakes hands with President-elect John F. Kennedy after accepting the Cabinet position of Defense Secretary (December 1960).

Donald H. Rumsfeld
(November 20, 1975—January 20, 1977)

Donald H. Rumsfeld was born July 9, 1932, in Chicago, Illinois. Rumsfeld received a bachelor's degree in politics from Princeton University in 1954. He then served three years as a Navy aviator and flight instructor before joining the Naval Reserve.

Rumsfeld was elected to the House of Representatives in 1962. He resigned from Congress to join the Nixon administration as Director of the Office of Economic Opportunity and a member of the Cabinet. In February 1973, he was appointed U.S. Ambassador to NATO in Brussels. After Richard Nixon resigned in 1974, he was called back to Washington, D.C., to head President Gerald Ford's transition team.

Rumsfeld became Ford's White House Chief of Staff and one of Ford's closest associates and advisors. When he was sworn in as Secretary of Defense, he was, at age 43, the youngest person to assume that office.

Rumsfeld brought much experience and knowledge to the Pentagon. He was a military veteran. He knew federal government finance and accounting. And he was familiar with NATO. But Rumsfeld's full potential was never realized. Ford lost the 1976 election, and a new Cabinet was eventually installed.

Donald Rumsfeld works in his White House office after being confirmed as Defense Secretary by the Senate (November 1975).

Caspar W. Weinberger
(January 21, 1981—November 23, 1987)

Caspar W. Weinberger was born in San Francisco on August 18, 1917. He earned a bachelor's degree from Harvard College in 1938. Then he received a law degree from Harvard Law School in 1941.

Weinberger joined the Army Infantry as a private. He served in the Pacific as a member of General Douglas MacArthur's intelligence staff. By the time he was released from duty, Weinberger was a captain. He worked as a law clerk, then joined a San Francisco law firm where he became a partner in 1959.

In 1968, Weinberger was appointed Director of Finance in Governor Ronald Reagan's California administration. Then in 1970, President Richard Nixon called Weinberger to Washington to be Chairman of the Federal Trade Commission. By 1973, Weinberger was Secretary of the Department of Health, Education, and Welfare where he remained until his resignation in 1975.

President Reagan nominated Weinberger to be Secretary of Defense. He had the ability to pry large increases in defense spending out of Congress. Weinberger also won support for U.S. military policies overseas. Because of Weinberger's many successes, he served as Secretary of Defense longer than anyone except Robert McNamara.

Defense Secretary Caspar Weinberger announces his resignation at the White House while President Ronald Reagan looks on (November 5, 1987).

Glossary

Campaign
A series of actions a person undertakes to attain a political goal.

Debate
A formal discussion or argument.

Deficit
The amount by which a sum of money falls short of the required amount.

Democrat
A member of the Democratic Party.

Economy
The management of a country's resources.

Independent
A person not associated with any established political party.

Media
The means of mass communication, such as newspapers, magazines, radio, and television.

National Debt

The total financial obligations of a national government.

Political Parties

Political organizations, such as the Democratic and Republican parties.

Primary

A meeting of registered voters of a political party for the purpose of nominating candidates.

Republican

A member of the Republican Party.

Connect With Books

Almanac of American Presidents: From 1789 to the Present. Facts on File, 1991.

Alotta, Robert. *A Look at the Vice Presidency.* Julian Messner, 1981.

Beard, Charles Austin. *The Presidents in American History: George Washington to George Bush.* Julian Messner, 1989.

Blassingame, Wyatt. *The Look-It-Up Book of Presidents.* Random House, 1990.

Degregorio, William A. *The Complete Book of U.S. Presidents: From George Washington to George Bush.* Barricade Books (New York), 1991.

Feerick, John D. *The First Book of Vice Presidents.* Franklin Watts, 1977.
The Vice Presidents of the United States. Franklin Watts, 1973.

Freidel, Frank. *The Presidents of the United States of America.* White House Historical Association, 1989.

Lengyel, Cornel Adam. *Presidents of the United States.* Golden Press, 1977.

Parker, Nancy Winslow. *The President's Cabinet and How It Grew.* Harper Collins, 1991.

Powers of the Presidency. *Congressional Quarterly,* 1989.

Index

Continued on page 32

Index (continued)

DATE DUE			

921
Asp

Italia, Robert

The Secretary of
Defense through Les
Aspin

Anderson Elementary

 GUMDROP BOOKS - Bethany, Missouri